Save Yourself from Foreclosure Handbook

Zunicorn Publishing
975 Brown St.
Akron, Ohio 44311

Contact us at: 330.773.7930
Email: Frank830@aol.com

ISBN: 1-4196-8799-9
ISBN-13: 978-1419687990

Save Yourself from Foreclosure Handbook
The PLAIN TRUTH

Frank Ruggiero

2008

Save Yourself from Foreclosure Handbook

Introduction

This book was written to answer the question "Foreclosure? What can I do?"

It is my attempt to help those who are filled with fear and have no idea what they can do about it. It is my hope that this book will help you to better understand the foreclosure process and your options to get out of it. This book is created from a homeowner's point of view and the results he can achieve if he acts quickly and decisively. It is written from the mind of a seasoned real estate investor who has been involved in many of these situations. I am a former licensed real estate agent and also a former licensed mortgage broker. I have owned dozens of properties over the years. Much of the discussions will be based on my twenty years experience in the housing industry dealing with buyers, sellers, lenders, courts, tenants, mortgage brokers, real estate agents and attorneys. I will try to communicate as much of this as I can in "laymen's terms", using only the most necessary real estate and legal jargon.

The information in this book is designed to answer general questions and give general advice about the foreclosure process. When reading this book, be aware that the advice, information, and/or forms were created to assist readers with general issues, not specific situations and as such does not replace the advice or representation of an attorney. I have not gone into lengthy and detailed descriptions regarding any of these possible actions you can use to stay out of foreclosure. I have provided you the seeds to examine for you and your attorney to discuss. These are not new ideas and techniques of dealing with property, but they may be new ideas to you, and a chance to save yourself.

If you desire detailed information or a strategy to accomplish your specific goals, or you would like me to talk with your attorney regarding your unique situation, feel free to contact me.

I cannot guarantee as to whether the use of this information will achieve the results you desire, only you can.

Realize that there are exceptions to every rule. Each foreclosure and bankruptcy case is unique unto itself just like a home loan or an individual.

It is assumed throughout this book that if you can avoid a foreclosure, then you should do so for you and your family's benefit.

Certain other assumptions are made regarding the reader of this book such as he understands the basics of a loan (i.e. interest, late charges, loan balance, etc.).

What we call a "lender" in this book is any type of a normal bank, savings and loan, credit union, local or national institution that lends money for mortgage loans. It can also be whomever it is that holds your mortgage (a friend, a relative or an acquaintance you bought your house from). I will simply refer to them as" lender" , "him", or "he".

Equity (the difference between the value of the property and the amount owed on it) will not be discussed using any specific figures for several reasons. Not every situation will have substantial amounts of equity in it. In any given case we can assume that if there is any equity in it, it is also in jeopardy by virtue of the foreclosure. It is up to you to determine if there is any equity to be concerned about, and if there is any, how to go about salvaging it.

Financing is defined as the limitless ways you can put together the money needed (purchase, sale or reinstatement money) to get the job done. It will usually refer to ways you can create or borrow money to fix the foreclosure.

I will attempt to show you how this can be done in several ways. You need to decide how much you can give-up and still come out satisfied with the results at the end of the process. If you decide not to give up any amount of equity to get a resolution, then you will have diminished your chances drastically to succeed. You must understand that you will probably not get all you want out of this, but if you can get the foreclosure resolved, we have accomplished our purpose of this book.

This book was not written to provide you with a solid understanding of the areas mentioned above (financing, equity, interest, loans, etc.). It is not written to provide you with step-by-step actions to repair your credit (which you will inevitably have to do) or to teach you how to budget your finances. Such information on any of these subjects is readily available in the mountains of books and articles already published in hard format and/or online.

Chapter 1
Don't Panic

The foreclosure process can be an extremely stressful, embarrassing, and intimidating time for the average homeowner. The vast majority of homeowners facing foreclosure have usually only purchased one home in their lifetime, the home they are now in and now they visualize it being taken from them, even "forcefully" if necessary.

Psychological Impact

Foreclosures come with their own set of unique and sometimes very frightening array of emotions and reactions that you may or may not experience at one time or another. (Let's hope you don't.). These include general panic, denial of or attempt to distance the problem, shock, remorse, anger, depression, numbness, embarrassment, possible anxiety attacks, or worse, not to mention many sleepless nights. If you're not a good crisis manager, you are in for a trip (an experience).

Remember, it is up to you how you will handle this important challenge.

<u>Realize that the outcome of this is entirely in your control</u>, if you learn the facts of foreclosure, make educated decisions based on the facts and take the appropriate action immediately. In this situation it is important that you understand all of your options available to you. Realize as this unfolds before you, you will always have options to resolve the issue before it is over, depending on your knowledge of what is taking place, what outcome you intend to pursue, and how quickly you pursue it.

Most likely you will react to it as you would with any other major turning point in your life. Hopefully, that is with an attitude of calmness, confidence, and patience. Freaking out isn't gonna do you any good. One of my real estate guru's used to say "eat the elephant one bite at a time."

One thing you need to do quickly, to assure yourself some time to consider this matter in full, is to "<u>answer your summons/complaint of foreclosure</u>" delivered to you by hand or by certified mail from the county you reside in, within the time specified (usually 28 days). You have the legal right to do this for yourself, without paying an expensive attorney, and you should. You can do this with a simple paragraph or two stating that you disagree with the complaint and some of the facts contained therin. Mail it to the clerk of courts, including your case number, name and address, and also send a copy to the plaintiff's attorney. Having done so, it lets the court and the lenders know that you are considering taking this further to trial. This can and will extend the amount of time you have to formulate your plan to deal with this matter. Hopefully you received this book at this point, or sooner.

Many times, if you do not respond to the notice, the court not having received an answer to the summons they sent you, can decide to render a judgment by default against you. You could lose the fight and never get to argue or attempt to fix it. Telling the court you don't have the money to fight the foreclosure won't help stop or slow it down either.

Most people envision foreclosure as starting by having missed some payments, and then they begin to avoid any attempts by the lender to contact them, while they are hoping to catch up. Next they see a "notice of default" that was filed with the county and being handed to them by the sheriff or an officer of the court. The owner has a chance to make-up the back payments and late fees to solve the problem, or the matter goes further towards a sheriff sale. Usually the homeowner reacts in a panicked knee-jerk fashion. If the lender is not able to find a workable solution for you (usually within 90-120 days past due), they "package up" your file information and send it to the attorney firm they have hired to deal with their foreclosure cases. It is at this point the lender decides it will now involve costs to regain the money or property back. His attorney bills him and that expense adds onto your total amount owed called legal fees. These will become a negotiable item as everything else is from this point on. You may be able to negotiate the legal fees down or pay none at all, depending on your situation.

At the sale the homeowner or anyone else can bid to purchase the house from the bank for the amount owed. If they are the highest bidder, they will get the home. If not, the bank will take possession (take back) of the property and try to sell again at a later date.

After the sale, the sheriff will have the deed transferred to the new owner or bank and may come to evict you and your family. On the appointed day, if you have not already left, they will actually set your possessions out on the street.

If the property is worth less than the total amount you owe on the mortgage loan, a deficiency judgment (another separate legal process) could be pursued against you. You could still owe your lender additional money (the deficiency) even after losing your home. He could possibly seek to gain control over any other assets (valuables) you have in order to satisfy the debt, and possibly even garnish your wages.

Quick Facts Regarding Foreclosure

<u>1.) Stay in contact with your lender</u> and be honest with him about your situation <u>if you intend to fix it.</u>

<u>2.) Foreclosures usually take months.</u> Realize that there are no quick solutions unless you can come up with all the cash needed all at once to get the loan back on track.

<u>3.) You do not need to abandon your home.</u> Only an order from the court can force you to leave your home. You may wind up being evicted, but there are procedures within the laws and the court system that the mortgage holder must follow for the foreclosure first, and then another set for the eviction process. From the time of missing your first payment to the time of the sheriff's sale, can easily be six months or more. This time is dependent on a lot of other factors such as which particular state you reside in, and how heavy a case load the courts have before yours. It will also depend on how aggressively your lender will pursue your case.

<u>4.) Scammers, liars, thieves abound like sharks</u> in the ocean ready to take advantage of the often confused and embarrassed homeowner. When your "notice of default" is filed at the county courthouse and because of the legal nature of the matter, your name and address may become part of public information offered through the court system and wind up being published in certain newspapers and publications (legal news, foreclosure lists, etc.). There are many groups of people and individuals who make their living working with people in this situation. Some are decent, ethical people, some are not.

<u>5.) Do not sign over your deed to someone</u>, or at least realize it does not relieve you from the responsibility of paying the mortgage, unless the new buyer was qualified by your lender and you have a signed release from the lender.

<u>6.) Never sign documents you don't fully understand.</u> Get any agreements or promises in writing, especially if you decide to give away your home. There are times you should and should not.

7.) <u>Explore all alternatives.</u> Realize if it sounds too good to be true, it probably is.

8.) <u>Losing your home to foreclosure will probably damage your credit.</u> If it does, and for how long depends on you.

9.) <u>Realize that panic, fear, or embarrassment are your enemies,</u> even though it may be what you are currently feeling. The tendency to close up (not talk with the involved parties or other people) at this time is also another ineffective way to deal with the issues.

There are many groups of people and individuals who make their living working with people in a foreclosure situation. Among them are:

A) Other lenders/ mortgage brokers- who are willing to refinance (give you a new loan) to replace the old one if there is enough equity (your part of the house you paid for) to allow it. If there is a considerable difference in the amount owed on it and the amount it would sell for, lenders will loan on it.

B) Attorneys- Bankruptcy and foreclosure attorneys will send you letters and mailers letting you know they are ready and willing to help you with this matter. If you don't find them first through friends or the yellow pages they usually find out about you through the legal publications and listings of new foreclosures, law suits, divorces, etc. printed weekly or more often.

C) Mortgage/loss mitigation negotiators- people who represent themselves as professionals who can save you from foreclosure. They may call themselves counselors or debt coordinators or other things, and usually they offer you their saving expertise for a fee. There are times when these people can be used to resolve a particular situation, depending on your decisions on what to do about the entire predicament you are now facing.

D) Private lenders/Investors- these are people who will work with the homeowner to arrange a new home loan for you in spite of you having been turned down from other lenders. Their rates (interest) will be higher than conventional rates for a normal buyer but if you shop around and look at all the loan products available to you, you can find a good competitive rate among them.

Investors will come in and try to buy the house from you. Be very cautious of what anyone proposes to do for you while in foreclosure and what they want for themselves. Usually, if it sounds too good to be true, it is. There is nothing wrong with anyone making a profit in helping you with your problem if you understand and agree to what they propose.

E) Your own Lender- your own lender will solicit you to arrange getting the loan back on track. If your loan is a government backed mortgage (FHA, VA, etc.) the lender may be required to offer alternatives to foreclosure to you through his own company or third party company such as Mortgage Outreach Service Company or others.

F) Crooks and scammers- this group of people includes those who will take your money and promise to save your house and/or your credit. Some provide the barest minimum of service on your behalf, some do nothing whatsoever to help you. Others are so unscrupulous that they would take your money and simply refer you to attorneys in the area who handle foreclosures. There are also those who would take your home from you by deceiving you and having you sign legal documents which allow them to even charge you rent while you reside there or evict you from the home you just gave to them.

G) Real Estate Agents- the agents represent the sellers before the foreclosure and then represent the bank when the property is taken back by them and later put on the market for sale.

H) Clean-up,clean- out,repair, maintenance crews- all these individuals and more are paid to do some type of work or service related to the property.

An equivalent flow of money occurs in the process when a home is sold so that a real estate transaction benefits many in the community and the city and county governments too.

Usual Causes of Foreclosure

Divorce
Forced transfer
Can't afford payments
Payments out of control due to adjustable rate
Loss of job
Unforeseen death of significant other
Failing business
Inherited with a mortgage in place
Built new house or outgrown old house but didn't sell yet
Too old to maintain the property.
Bankruptcy
Major lawsuit pending
Predatory loan
Unforeseen medical issues/ bills
Bad tenants
Serious car accident
Miscellaneous causes

Chapter 2
What is it?

Definition of foreclosure

Foreclosure is the legal process that a lender can use to repossess (take back) your home. It is the lenders attempts to recover money and or collateral promised to them if you fail to make the payments agreed on in signing your note and mortgage.

Foreclosure can also occur on a loan for which you used your house as collateral (a home equity loan). They can also happen in some contract for deed sales (land contracts). I have seen cases occur many times when the property belongs to an estate of a deceased person. None of the family continued to make the payments, and the lender forecloses. Any and all actions the lender takes to accomplish this is called the foreclosure process.

When you have fallen behind or missed consecutive payments on your mortgage, foreclosure may occur. IT DOES NOT have to occur. In fact, it is entirely up to you and will be determined by how accurately and honestly you assess your situation.

What is happening here??

As I stated above, foreclosure is the legal process your lender can use to repossess (take back) your home. The lender never really had the home to begin with, but basically he gave you the money to purchase the property and secured your agreement to repay the money with the terms of the note you signed at closing. He then created a mortgage which secured that monetary loan to that particular property.

Most people never read the entire note and or mortgage documentation when buying their home. It is usually among the myriads of papers, affidavits, and disclosures that are all part of the "closing" or bringing to execution the transfer of real property from one person to another.

Contained within the mortgage and the notes are certain statements (clauses) that were agreed upon between you and the lender. For example, contained within the note were placed statements as to how the note would be paid back in full, when payments would be considered due, the amount of each payment, etc. Most of the clauses contained in the mortgage and note may have seemed too wordy and tedious, but now having failed to keep up your end of the agreement, and being foreclosed on, certain clauses now become very important.

One of these clauses affecting you in foreclosure is the acceleration clause, which is contained in the note you signed. It basically says if you fail to pay the lender as agreed upon herein, the lender can demand that the full amount of the balance is now due, (bank calling the loan due) plus back interest, plus late charges, plus any and all accrued legal fees in working with your delinquent status be paid in full all at once and immediately. If in the very unusual case that you had a very small amount of debt on your loan to pay-off, you could simply write a check or perhaps use your credit card to pay the outstanding amount, thus solving the foreclosure altogether. Rarely is it that simple.

Once your first payment is missed, by not being paid on the due date or during the grace period provided, you are technically in default of your home loan. I doubt there are any lenders (including yours) that would begin such a costly project as a foreclosure on someone who is only a few days late beyond the grace period. Even if the lender was ruthless enough to take it to court, a judge would probably throw the case out.

However, by you not making your payment in the agreed fashion, this certainly attracts the attention of the lender (or his computer). Your account is then singled out and placed in non-payment status. Being earmarked as such, your account will soon be noticed by either a computer or a human or both, depending on the size of your lender. He, she or it will be assigned to deal with this delinquency. Usually you will begin to receive written or telephone attempts to contact you regarding the unpaid amount.

If you simply "forgot" to pay it, the "gentle" letter or call may suffice. The lender thanks you for your prompt attention, receives your late fee along with your payment, and wishes you a good day. If your situation is not quite that easy to solve then the more serious side of the issue rapidly becomes apparent. Your lender will begin to question you as to the reason for being late. He may also probe you for information to see if this occurrence is a one-time fixable delay of payments, or if he can see that additional payments left on loan is in jeopardy. From now on until as long as he can, the lender will attempt to contact you to get the payments made to bring the loan current, thus, finding a solution. He may find one you both can live with. He may not.

In most cases of such delinquency it would be to the lenders advantage to work towards a solution, rather than spend large amounts of time and money, with usually poor results, and foreclose on you. I think many banks are beginning to recognize this as an efficient and cost-productive way to work with many homeowners.

The important thing to remember is that a payment missed brings attention and begins the lender contact procedures, which in reality is an attempt to gauge the viability of the loan's future.

Obviously, missing the second payment in a row will draw increased interest in your situation. For the vast majority of the lenders out there, usually the action/decision stage is triggered after missing the third payment (90 days past due). And certainly by missing the fourth you can be sure a plan of action is being formulated against you to get back what is due them. This is when they package you up and ship you to the attorney.

Now is when you too should already begin to formulate your strategy.

Generic Pre-foreclosure Process

A) Owner misses mortgage payment

B) Late notice sent and/or phone contact attempted by the lender to contact the owner

C) Owner misses additional payments and doesn't contact the lender

D) Bank continues to attempt to contact owner through mail and phone calls and resolve the delinquency

E) No arrangements are agreed upon and owner continues to miss payments

F) Bank issues to the homeowner a demand for payment in full. This means the entire amount of the balance is due, plus any late charges, and back interest on the loan. If the delinquency continues a much larger amount will be added to the total. It is the legal fees the lender will pay to have an attorney to handle the foreclosure process. They can be any amount, usually initially $1-4k, but they can get even higher. All these expenses are added to your loan to increase the amount you must pay in full to rectify this debt.

G) No communication or resolution is coordinated with the lender and the property goes through the court towards a date the sheriff sets to sell the property at a public auction.

Generic Legal Foreclosure Process

A) Owner misses mortgage payments.

B) Bank notifies owner of Notice of Intent to Foreclose by sheriff and/ or certified mail.

C) Bank commences action in courts to foreclose.

D) Legal notices are made as required by law to be published in accepted papers (legal news, etc.).

E) No payment arrangement made with the bank and the required notice and waiting periods expire.

F) Court holds hearing regarding the parties claims.

G) Court issues order which allows bank to foreclose.

H) Legal notice published in accepted papers of actual foreclosure sale.

I) No resolution, settlement or work-out reached with bank.

J) House sells at sheriff's sale to the highest bidder.

Only after reviewing your particular situation can you make an informed decision. That decision should be based on your income, expenses, your total assets and liabilities, and predominately the underlying reason why you are presently in foreclosure. It will also be based upon what type of mortgage you currently have or are still able to obtain. Additional factors that come into play are where in the foreclosure process you are, and when/if you decide what to do with the house (keep it or let it go).

Now that you understand a little better some of your options that you have to deal with this pressing and worrisome problem, let us discuss some of the considerations in determining what to do.

Chapter 3
Determining what to do

I started this book with chapter 1 being called "Don't Panic!!" My thinking was that most people that are buying and reading this book are already feeling panicky or on their way there. I wanted to address the panic issue in the first few pages to let you know <u>it is entirely up to you what you do from here!</u>

By reading this book you will have a much better idea of most if not all of the possible ways out of foreclosure! <u>All statements in this book are being made with the homeowner's outcome being most important.</u>

Foreclosure is a very complex topic, if you don't think so ask any attorney. Don't worry, he won't say too much about it (for free), even though he may deal with it every day. Millions are paid by lenders each year to law firms being used as just another business tool by lenders in the housing industry every day.

Their job is to resolve the matter of acquiring either the collateral (house) and/or the money that is due the lender through the legal processes. They are not wicked or evil people but they have got a job to perform. Contrary to how you feel right this moment, your lender is not a heartless machine either, no matter how much he/it acts like one.

The problem with lenders is most of them are large institutions and/or corporations in other states or locations that are far removed from knowing anything about you, your life and your situation. Yes, they have your data on a computer in front of them, but usually you are just another account among thousands that are delinquent.

In comparison, having your loan through a local lender or a private individual has some benefits as well as pitfalls. One benefit is that if the lender is small enough that you actually know the bank/branch manager, you can walk in to meet with him to discuss your current situation. He may be willing to give you extra consideration because of the personal contact he has had with you. However, knowing you personally, he may dislike something about you and build up a vendetta against you. Usually local banks such as these have a positive base from "knowing" the customer which to begin resolving the foreclosure. Sadly not enough foreclosures fall into this category.

To extremely simplify matters we can look at a lender as a group of people who are good people just like you. They took some of their hard earned money and pooled this together (thru a bank, savings, and 401k's) with others. They tried to make a better life for themselves and/or their families by lending their money out in the form of home loans to help other people buy their own home, and to profit thereby from their actions.

However, do not be misled by this picture of how it works. If in the event you cannot make your payments and are foreclosed on, remember, no one individual will ever suffer from this foreclosure more than you.

What can/should I Do?

Foreclosure should also be a time to step back and look at the true reality of your personal situation. You will have a greater chance to remedy your problem if you acknowledge that there is a crisis and act on it before it gets to be overwhelming rather than continue to deny it. You should review your personal matters as to where you are now financially, and emotionally. Did you realize what you were doing when you did it and know why you were doing it? What previous actions or inactions have you taken that inevitably brought you to this point in life? Were they appropriate? Did you learn anything from what has occurred?

Hopefully at this critical point you can be honest with yourself when sorting matters out. You should accept the responsibility of your thinking and your actions, in the past, now, and in the future.

If you had clear intentions at the outset of this loan to be honorable and honest in your actions, (no fraudulent intent), and the goal was to improve the quality of you/your family's life and you did, then there is no shame to bear. Millions of hard working, diligent people are thrown into foreclosure for many reasons beyond their control. Many times it had nothing to do with their financial or budgeting knowledge or lack of.

Analyze your individual situation from a financial, emotional (which includes social) and practical point of view.

From a financial perspective.

Make an assessment of your financial situation. Consider all of your income and all of your financial obligations to see if you can afford to continue to pay your current mortgage, or if you need another option. The forms in Chapter 9 can better assist you gauge your finances. Ask yourself can I continue to keep this home? After you have a good understanding of your financial situation, what you can and cannot afford, you will learn what to do with your home. You will need to make a decision on whether your priority will be to keep your home or let it go.

From an emotional perspective

From an emotional perspective you will find that being in foreclosure feels as if everyone is looking at you and knows all about your predicament. All kinds of people, usually strangers will try to communicate with you about your foreclosure situation. You may feel embarrassed, humiliated, angry or even ashamed because you fell behind on your payments. This may or may not happen to you.

If it does it may take some time to overcome these feelings during and after the foreclosure process. Talk these feelings out with whomever you feel comfortable with to get beyond them. Remember, thousands of others throughout the country are facing very similar scenarios or worse.

Sometimes it is easy to make a decision based on what we want or desire, but not see what the consequences of that decision might be, therefore we need to think them through carefully. This is increasingly difficult to do if we are talking about the family home for twenty years or more, the one that mom or dad or yourself has grown up in. Saving it may involve getting extraordinary help from family, friends, or even colleagues because of the sentimental value.

Harsh as it may sound, if there is not family heritage yet established in connection to this property (you've only owned it for one or two years), it is easier to understand that when this one is gone, another home will replace it.

From a Practical Perspective

It would be wise to make a smart and informed decision that will benefit all parties involved with your home.

One thing that will occur is that your credit rating will take a nose-dive downward because of missed house payments.

Once this happens it will take time to correct this problem too and you should be willing to accept that consequence.

Mostly, you will need to assess your current and future ability in paying your mortgage to determine if this is a temporary condition in your life that will soon correct itself or if this is really a long term problem that will be with you for some time to come. For example, if you are in foreclosure because of a temporary job loss, you may need to realize when you do return to work you may have to take a lower paying job thus affecting your ability to continue to pay the mortgage.

After looking at this from all the perspectives and in a realistic manner, you should be able to determine a course of action regarding your foreclosure. The truth about foreclosure is that there is only 2 possible outcomes, but many variations of them. They are:

Do Nothing
OR
Fight To Keep

The following chapters will deal with each possibility separately in an attempt to present the reader with the various options and possible consequences of each action.

Maximize the experience you have before you. It is important you come away from this having learned some lessons, be they financial or otherwise, or you will be doomed to repeat them or something similar in the future. If in the event you need financial information, there are a multitude of services available to anyone who wants to develop a budget or a system for dealing with their finances. Today with internet access you can locate many by simply typing in "budget" in the search bar. Contact your local and community agencies for additional information.

As I stated in the introduction to this book, my purpose of this book is not to structure your budget for you, that responsibility is and always has been yours.

Many reading this book may well know how to budget, and find themselves in this situation because of other causes, one of them being from an attempt to "invest in real estate". If that is the case and you have been paying attention you certainly have learned some thing's not to do again!

That, kind person, is experience.

Remember that most others who have failed before they succeeded, Lincoln, Edison, Trump, Madonna......Almost all of the great scientists, achievers, current real estate tycoons, leading businessmen, and actors have failed miserably before achieving their successes.

It's how we learn.

Chapter 4
Do Nothing / Let it Go

When faced with an apparent foreclosure looming on the horizon, this is certainly one option.

Unfortunately, I see this option chosen by a large number of people, usually by default or inaction. To deny the problem exists or bury your head in the sand like an ostrich may get you through the situation, but you will have very little control over the final outcomes. But if you intend to do nothing or walk away, you may not care.

In a strategy of do nothing or walk away the best possible outcome that can happen is that the lender forecloses on the property and having accomplished that, they take the property back, leave you alone and you never pay another penny. Also, they forget to notify your credit bureau of your delinquency and decide not to notify Uncle Sam that they have forgiven your debt. Dream on.

On the other hand, the worst that can happen is that through the legal process they take everything that you own including your house, your cash, your car, your furniture, your pets, and any other assets that you own (family members don't count). If that amount still does not satisfy the debt, they can attempt to attach your wages (garnishment) where you work.

One thing to keep in mind with the "do nothing strategy" is that you can always decide during the foreclosure process to change your strategy and become willing to communicate with your lender.

For our purposes, "do nothing" means the same as "walk away". Both concepts mean not contacting the bank to inform them about your decisions, action or inaction about the property. Other terms used are "let it go" (the house) or "give it up".

It is up to you as to what degree you decide to participate in these or any matters. Any amount of participation will allow you and the bank to begin to negotiate and/or work out a resolution.

Certain events will continue to happen with or without your participation.

Some type of notice will come to the house from the bank announcing their intentions to foreclose whether you are still occupying it or not. You may have already left the residence months ago. Most lenders once having turned over your delinquent account to their attorneys will proceed with the legal process even if they never hear from you again. The process is designed to work with or without your input into it.

Almost all banks will eventually send someone to the property to check on its condition. If not already secured, the banks representative will secure the house to avoid any unauthorized entry. Sometimes, when the lender is in another state, or swamped with a large number of foreclosures to handle, it will take a while before someone comes to check on the house. Many times it is the local health department who actually secures the property. If entry has been gained through a broken window or an unlocked door, they usually put boards on all the first floor windows and doors to prevent further access. The monetary cost charged by either the city or the county to do this is added onto the tax bill as an assessment against the property and eventually paid by the bank or new buyer.

When people abandon a property the grass continues growing creating a noticeable eyesore in the neighborhood. In my locality, a health dept. agent may visit the property and places a tag on it notifying the owners to cut the grass. If after a certain period of time since being tagged, no one cuts the grass, a crew of workers will be sent to the property to cut it. When this occurs it will also be added to the property taxes, as an assessment and usually is expensive.

If you have decided to move out, and try and forget the house, it may haunt you for a long time. Some people decide to do just that. I have seen many times where people leave all or most of their possessions in the house, lock it, or not, and don't come back. In these cases, the real estate companies handling those properties, when/if the bank takes possession, will have the personal items and trash removed. There are many times a private buyer from the bank may clean-out the house themselves. I have also seen buyers buy the house with all the contents included and sell it to another buyer who intends to rehab the property. It matters little what you decide to leave behind. People who do this obviously don't care about these items. Usually anything of value has already been taken and/or sold. What's left will be picked over by those assigned to clean-out the house, or anyone who may gain access to the house before that.

In lower income neighborhoods vacant or abandoned homes are usually 'noticed' by those in the area within four to six weeks or sooner. Tell tale signs such as newspapers lying around, over stuffed mailboxes, untouched door flyers or miscellaneous tags accumulate around the front door. Yards with tall grass and overgrown bushes are an indicator no one is there.

In situations like these many times the house will be entered by strangers, vandalized, damaged or even set afire.

Also, many times people angry and frustrated that they are losing their home sometimes destroy their homes before leaving it feeling that they are making the lender suffer for his actions. They will do many things like destroy drywall or remove walls, remove cabinets, take the fixtures, copper, furnace, water heater, air conditioning units, windows and even the light bulbs!

If able to be proven, the homeowner can technically be held responsible for any damage/destruction that has been done to the property. Again, it is a question if whether the time and money spent in the pursuit will justify the results.

From my point of view, this is not necessary and should not be done. It is not the lenders fault that you cannot make the payments that you agreed to at the beginning of the loan.

In fact, the homeowner can and usually does get away with this destroying of the property. It is usually not discovered until after he has left. All too often the words, "it wasn't like that when I left it" are used to dismiss the homeowner of any responsibility.

The condition the home is left in and the repair of it will become the responsibility of the new buyer. If you destroy the property before leaving, it will translate to a longer time before it resells and a lower price at the time of sale.

Many people move out, go to another location and try to forget about their loan or mortgage.

The problem is that their credit information follows them wherever they go. Owners who do nothing but leave the premises are often surprised when months later they are sued by their lenders for money which is still due (the deficiency) even after the Sheriff's sale of the home.

If the amount earned at the sale is not enough to satisfy the amount owed to the bank, the bank may proceed in attempting to collect the difference (deficiency) from the used-to-be homeowner through a deficiency judgment. Rarely is this done because this too requires additional money spent by the bank after the foreclosure is done for additional attorney fees and court filings, in an attempt to collect money from the homeowner, who has already shown he cannot pay.

Many banks have learned to cut their expenses by simply sending a form 1099 to the individual and to the U.S. government which tells Uncle Sam that they have forgiven the homeowners debt and that the homeowner should be taxed on the forgiven amount, as if it were a cash gift to the homeowner.

This "gift" that is forgiven is usually thousands of dollars that the government will tax the homeowner on. The lender writes off the debt in their taxes and must not attempt to further collect the debt after reporting it.

In fact, this situation is so prevalent that the Internal Revenue Service has recently added a new section to its website to answer tax questions for those losing their homes because of foreclosure. The new section on IRS.gov includes a worksheet to help homeowners determine whether they are eligible for any foreclosure-related tax relief. For those who find they owe additional tax, it includes a form for requesting a payment agreement with the IRS!

The IRS also noted that if the debt wiped out through foreclosure exceeds the value of the property, the difference is normally taxable income. But there is a special rule that allows insolvent borrowers to offset that income to the extent their liabilities exceeds their assets. President Bush, in an attempt to deal with the foreclosure crisis has proposed tax relief for homeowners. He said he would support a temporary tax law change to let homeowners avoid paying taxes on forgiven debt in loans that are being restructured by the various lenders. This should give both homeowners and lenders some more incentive to modify the loan or otherwise workout a resolution.

The most intelligent way to prevent or resolve a foreclosure issue is to maintain with the lender some kind of communication and cooperation, and the "Do nothing" strategy should only be used as a last resort.

There are many other ways in which to finalize this issue so that you are not plagued by it forever. Talking with your lender may bring some results you both can live with.

Chapter 5
Fight to Keep

Life altering occurrences can happen to anyone at any time. These changes can force us to fall behind in our monthly payments. If we miss our credit card payments it affects our credit rating. If we miss our home loan payments, it affects not only our credit rating, but our home too. The lender can take the home.

If you are still reading this book then you are considering keeping your home or your property. This book will attempt to show you many if not all the ways in which you can. Or you may not want to keep the home but also you don't feel it to be right for you to just give-up, do nothing, or walk away. This book will also show you some liquidation options that are available to a homeowner.

There are two ways the claim (interest) that you have in your home may be terminated in a foreclosure matter, by consent or by the courts (a judge).

If you consent (agree) to sign the deed to the home over to the lender, your rights to the property are cancelled. Most lenders, upon accepting the deed, will not continue to seek any further restitution. You can have the lender put this in writing before you sign it over to them and I suggest you do just that.

If the lender files a foreclosure against you, asking the courts to award them the deed to the property, then a judge will be making the final decision.

The lender and the owner may agree together on any type of settlement or arrangement at any time before this, which would cancel the foreclosure process.

There are many facts regarding foreclosure that most homeowners are not aware of simply because this is usually a once-in-a-lifetime event for most of them. You didn't miss out on foreclosure class in high school.

One fact is lenders do not really desire to foreclose on delinquent borrowers. The time and expense to do this on each delinquent property is usually enormous. It costs a lender an average of $30,000 or more to foreclose on a home. It bogs down their payment receiving machine. A foreclosure is almost always a losing proposition for them.

WHY BANKS WANT YOU TO KEEP YOUR LOAN ON TRACK

Lenders primarily make their profit in making loans and receiving payments from them. When you look at a fully amortized loan from a bank and you calculate the total amount of payments made on a 30 year loan, you will pay nearly 3 times the amount of the purchase price of the home.

Here's an example:

$100,000 loan at 12% interest for 30 years = $1028.62 principal and interest payment. The major portion of your monthly payment goes toward interest with very little being applied to reducing the balance (principal) of the loan. Interestingly it is not until the end of the twenty-fourth year of this loan that more of your monthly payment is applied toward the principal than toward the interest.

You may find it surprising to know that the total interest paid on this loan over 30 years would be approx. $270,275.00.

$100,000.00 @   12% / 360 monthly payments (30 yrs)

= 1028.62 monthly payment (principle and interest)

= 370,303 total of payments

= 100,000 original amount borrowed

$270,303 in interest paid over the span (term) of 360 months

It is easy to see why a lender would want a loan to continue producing payments.

On the other hand, the lender has no other required course of action under the law to retrieve the money (or collateral) owed to them, if you can't or won't pay, unless you suggest some.

With the increasing amounts of foreclosures nationwide due to many factors, the Federal Reserve and other government agencies, even at state and local levels are working with lenders to offer more options to those behind on payments. This will result in even more people being able to work out a way to keep their homes.

The vast majority of homeowners are not even aware that most lenders themselves offer programs for those behind in their payments.

The single biggest mistake most borrowers make when they fall behind on their payments is NOT contacting the lender. You have to let them know that you are facing difficulties in making the payments if you have expectations of working this out.

Ideally, this should be done when you realize that you have missed one payment and are not going to be able to make the upcoming one either. Do not ignore the lenders and attempts to reach you. Always have a pad and paper to write down the name, number, department, extension, date and time of those you speak with. Tell the person on the other end of the line the reason for being late. If you are not able to catch-up the missed payment and get back to your regular schedule of paying on time, mention this to the lender. You will have determined by now, from the previous chapters, if this is a temporary problem or not before this conversation, so advise the lender of this. There are fixes for short-term (temporary) situations and for long-term situations. Ask the lender for his loss-mitigation department to help you determine which options are available for you to work this problem out. Calling the 800# the lender provides on your monthly statement is a good start

This is also a point where your pride, fear and or embarrassment can block your success. You must overcome all of these and deal with your lender in an honest and open manner.

If after considering your situation from all points of view, and deciding to keep your home, you will have to choose on how you will go about accomplishing this.

I have found that generally speaking, there are about six avenues available to you to fix a foreclosure. One of these, Do Nothing we spoke about in chapter 4. They all are listed below.

Do nothing
Your own options available to you
Your and/or another lenders options
Sell home to avoid foreclosure
Outside Sources
Bankruptcy

Some of these actions you can take on your own, some others you will need to hire professionals who specialize in these areas Use common sense in working with everyone. Ask questions so that you are aware of the different options that are available to you at any given step in the process.

When it comes to utilizing professionals to work with you in saving your home, try to choose people who have experience in their particular field and have dealt with these specific problems many times.

Your Own Options

Your own options (friends, relatives, associates, family, acquaintances, etc.) to save yourself from foreclosure will depend on your unique and particular circumstances in your life. You may have cash in your checking or savings that would allow you to catch-up the missed payments. You may be expecting a lump sum payment to come. You may have family or friends that would help you to get out of the temporary situation that you are in. You may have stocks that you can cash in to help meet the need for avoiding foreclosure. Life insurance plans or 401k's may allow you to borrow from them in times of emergencies.

For those of you who may have a home that is larger than you actually need, you may be able to rent out a part of it, either as an apartment if possible, or actually rent out the separate bedrooms with some house privileges to others. I have seen many people use this idea in order to help them generate additional income to catch-up back payments or use to help pay the current mortgage payment. There are times when you can rent out the extra space you have in the attic or garage to supplement the mortgage payment. You will need to sit down and assess your individual personal situation to determine if you can find some ways to avoid the foreclosure.

Your or another Lender's Options

Lender programs are broken down into two major categories: Liquidation programs and Retention programs.

Liquidation programs are designed to help those who cannot afford to stay in their home, but have not yet been able to sell it on the market. Many times homeowners realize that the burden of paying on the home is more than they can handle so they attempt to sell it on the market. They still try to keep up with the payments until it gets sold, usually tapping and draining any other kinds of cash or credit at their disposal. I have seen situations where people are being foreclosed on their first mortgage, and it is behind, yet they continue to pay on time on the second mortgage because it is the smaller of the two monthly payments they are required to make. If this is you, stop throwing your money away. Save it and the first mortgage payments as cash for your future living needs. This is a sad state because at this point they are only staving off the inevitable foreclosure and using up whatever resources that are left. Worse yet, they deal with a Real Estate agent who doesn't realize the gravity of the underlying financial situation and lists the house for near or more than market value which translates to a much longer time on the market and additional expense for the seller.

Most sellers don't realize they can put their own for-sale-by-owner sign out, and if they find a buyer and he is willing to pay all expenses, sell it to the buyer, not costing them anything out of pocket to have it done. No agent is really needed. If you have found a buyer, calling any title company will get you the help you need to walk through the deal cheaply. If necessary and you can afford to, you may be able to put some of your own cash in to make the sale happen and get the mortgage off your back.

If you are still not able to sell, the lender may offer you some help in the form of a short sale. A short sale may occur when the lender realizes that for whatever reason he may not be able to get back all of the money due to them. In such cases, the lender is willing to take a reduced amount for the property instead of the entire amount owed. You may be able to find someone interested in buying your place but not willing to pay the amount you owe the bank. If you present a bona fide offer to the lender he may be willing to take the reduced amount as a satisfaction of debt and cut his losses. You can usually arrange this type of sale with the lender yourself. Be certain to arrange within the sale a written agreement between you and your lender that the sale will completely satisfy the debt and no further action will be taken to recover any other money from you.

Retention programs are designed to work with you in keeping your home. They are usually offered by your own lender or even another lender.

If you are fortunate enough to have a "face-to-face" lender, as in a situation with someone you know who sold you his home with owner—financing where he created a note and mortgage for the transaction, you should realize that any agreement you and he settle upon, and put into writing (notarized, dated and signed by both parties) will supersede the earlier note and mortgage (agreement) and become the new contract or agreement for the property.

If you have missed two or three payments, you and the lender (face to face) can sit down and discuss what has been going wrong over the past few months. After an honest explanation of your present situation to him and your intentions toward the future of this loan (note) the lender may decide that with some changes made, the loan can continue to be a profitable investment for him. The lender, with your agreement, can modify the terms of the note if he decides to. He can lower the amount of interest charged on the loan, or extend the term of the loan for some months. He can have the buyer make only the interest portion of the payments for say, six to twelve months. Or he can suspend making the entire monthly payment for a period of time to allow the homeowner to get back on his feet. In fact, you and he can discuss several methods of catching up and even create a completely new note if you decide too. This is a vastly over-simplified example of a mortgage loan (home loan) but it does illustrate the degree of flexibility in the matter if both parties are working together to prevent a foreclosure.

For large institutions or corporations that handle thousands of mortgages and their monthly payments this would be almost impossible to accomplish. Still, from all the accounts that they do handle, they will always have a percentage that fall behind. Those will get personal attention from real lenders or their employees. Large lenders have set-up departments to deal with this, called collections and loss mitigation.

These departments review your situation in detail with you. That is their job. They try and update any information on you and ask questions to determine what options you may have to correct the delinquency. Usually, they will ask the borrower to fill out some current financial forms so they can get a more accurate picture of your current financial situation and compare that to what is was like when you first got your loan. It is to your advantage to be honest with the lender. If you make out your situation better than it really is, you may get an agreement that isn't going to work for you (payments too high, not enough time to catch-up), leaving you as bad off as you were, or worse. However, if you make your situation appear more drastic than it is, the lender may decide that he is only able to offer you liquidation options and not able to help you stay in the house.

Personal Options
Ask lender for more time to fix
Utilize any/all credit resources still available/lines of credit
Borrow from family or friends to reinstate
Borrow from stocks or 401k's
Borrow from insurance plans/retirement
Sale of other assets or personal property
Rent out some space in your home (bedroom, garage, attic)
Have someone assume your loan
Bankruptcy

Retention programs with Lenders include:
Forbearance Plans
Miscellaneous Repayment Plans
Loan Modification and/or refinance
Reinstatement
Partial Claims* VA or FHA loans
2nd mortgage

Liquidation programs with Lenders include:
Pre-foreclosure sale
Agent/Investor
Short sale/ reduced pay-off
Sell Yourself
Deed in lieu of foreclosure
Assumption

We will discuss each of the retention and liquidation items listed above to give you a better understanding of what each solution is and what each entails.

Lender retention Programs

Forbearance plan/ miscellaneous repayment plans-
This is usually an agreement between the lender and the borrower that gets the loan back on track through the payment of a lump sum or a schedule of payments over a period of time. For example, if a borrower is behind in their payments by $3000, the lender may allow the borrower to pay the money back through installment payments over six or twelve months. The lender can also allow the borrower to pay a reduced monthly payment until the borrower has an opportunity to get back on track and pay any remaining arrearages in one lump sum (like at tax return time, Christmas bonus, sales commission check). There is no set requirements to a forbearance plan or any of the miscellaneous repayment solutions you and the lender decide upon. After arriving on a solution you both are satisfied with, it is a good idea to get this agreement in writing from your lender to avoid any confusion as you follow the plan.

Mortgage modification—
A mortgage (loan) modification is a change in any of the terms of the original note. We briefly mentioned this in our

face-to-face lender scenario. One solution available is to add the past amount due into your existing loan, financing it over a longer period of time. This will extend your loan out for a longer amount of time than originally scheduled to be paid off, but does solve the delinquency and gets you back onto a normal payment plan. Generally, loan modification becomes an option when the borrower's income has been decreased and he is no longer able to make the payments at the former level, but will be able to keep the loan current with the lower payments after the modifications.

Reinstatement or refinance—

Reinstatement occurs when you are behind in your payments but you can promise to pay a lump sum to bring your payments current by a specific date. This works well if you are fortunate enough to have a sum of money that will be coming to you soon to use.

Refinancing is a condition in which the existing lender or another lender will allow the borrower to get a new loan to pay-off the current loan with late fees and costs rolled in to the new loan. For example, if the amount owed on the home is $60,000, but the house is worth $100,000, then a new lender can refinance for $70,000 paying off the old loan and giving you a new loan and payment amount that will make it easier for you to keep current. These refinancing options are offered to borrowers who are facing a setback in their finances and have shown an excellent credit history in the past, and can prove that they can support the new mortgage payment.

Partial Claim—

If your loan is a VA or FHA insured loan, your lender may be able to help you to apply for and receive a one-time payment from the VA or FHA to get your loan back to a current status. If your loan is of this type, you should ask them about their programs. You may be required to sign a promissory note which allows HUD to place an additional lien on your property for the amount received from them. This note is usually interest free, but must be repaid either when you finally pay-off your property or when you sell the property. I'm sure they have 800 phone numbers or websites.

Second mortgage—

There are times when the equity in your property justifies you being able to get a second or junior lien, in order to make up any back payments, late fees, and other charges necessary to reinstate the loan. The problem here is that the borrower will be required to make an additional (2nd) mortgage payment to cover the new loan along with his original obligation on the original (first) mortgage. Interest rates on second mortgage loans are usually somewhat higher than the rate on your first mortgage loan and the borrower should be aware of this and make sure this option is something he can do financially.

Lender Liquidation Programs

Pre-foreclosure sale

There are times when the above solutions are not available to you for one reason or another. It could be that you are unable to reinstate your loan and you are facing eminent foreclosure. At that point it may become clear that selling the property before foreclosure is completed, may be the only way out. This allows the borrower a chance to salvage his credit, pay-off the loan, keep and utilize any of the remaining equity in the home you get back to use for a new start.

For example, if $40,000 is owed on a home appraised at $80,000, it is possible to sell the property for something less than the appraised value, say $60,000, pay-off the loan, and use the remaining amount after expenses to start fresh at a new location.

One problem that arises in situations like is this that

the home owner tries to get the maximum amount for the property and in the process of hanging in there for top dollar, hangs himself by not accepting a realistic offer, notifying his lender of a buyer for the property, and allowing enough time for the deal to be closed before the Sheriff's sale date.

Don't let that happen to you. I can't tell you how many times I've seen people try to squeeze every last dime out of a property and lose everything because of their greed.

You need to realize that the clock is ticking and you are in a pressing situation regarding the foreclosure and entertain any reasonable offer presented to you that meets your minimum amount needed to cover expenses and allows you some cash to start fresh with.

Sell your home

There are four possible ways a homeowner in default and facing foreclosure may want to sell their home

Selling with an agent

This is the most common way houses are sold. However, in a foreclosure situation, it may not be the best way for a number of reasons.

First, let us hope you choose an agent that is not a friend or relative, or friend of a friend. They should be experienced and have a track record of sales in your neighborhood. Tell the agent you are facing foreclosure. Let him know how much cash you need to solve the foreclosure, and get some of your equity out. If the agent doesn't see your need to sell quickly, it could be disastrous. Ask the agent his opinion of market value, but use good sense in determining your asking price. The agent may argue that it is worth more than you are willing to sell at, but it is you who may wind up on the auction block if you ask too high a price. If your house is listed with an agent and he has not had any showings of the property, or offers on it after 45 days or more, you should ask to cancel the listing, and sell the property yourself through newspaper ads and or a for-sale-by-owner sign. Tell him this is what you intend to do up front so that he may put his best efforts forward immediately to sell the property, and if he doesn't, you can still part as friends. If the market is hot in your area while you are trying to sell, he should be able to get the job done. Tell him you want to be notified of all offers on the property to see if they might work. If repairs need done before selling, factor in those costs and give the buyer some discount in the asking price so that the house can be sold quickly.

Selling to an investor

Selling to an investor has some true advantages. Experienced investors can purchase your home very quickly as opposed to a traditional buyer. They usually can offer a fair price, thus helping you to save your credit and giving you the chance to walk away with some cash for a fresh start. The selling price is typically less, but there are no agent commissions, usually no home inspections, and very few if any buyer contingencies. As in any situation, you should be aware of what the facts are and decide if it is going to work for you. Realize you are not going to get everything you desire from this, but if it solves the problem for you, it may be the answer you need.

Sell via a "short sale" or a reduced pay-off

A short sale occurs when the homeowner and lender agree to sell the property for less than the amount owed on it. Although this can be a long process, one that requires considerable participation from you, it seems to be a very effective way to avoid a foreclosure and satisfy a lender.

It is a process best worked through with an investor or someone who has experience in doing short sales. In fact, there are companies created to do just that. They will handle all the details needed to present to your lender a complete package of the information he will need to determine if he will accept the short sale offer or not. Many factors will be considered such as your current financial picture, your explanation of what has occurred to cause this problem, the condition of the property (whether it is in good shape or not, i.e. marketable) and other factors gathered during the information update process.

One thing to keep in mind when trying to do a short sale is that if the lender agrees to take less than what is owed to him, he most certainly will not allow the homeowner to make any profit in this type of deal, or to get any cash for his equity. You simply liquidate the house for the agreed on amount and the lender takes all the cash.

Sell the house yourself

This seems to be a very practical way to deal with the property although many people will say they can't sell the house themselves. Actually, it can be as simple as putting a for-sale-by-owner-sign out in the yard. Or, you may choose to spend some money in advertising the property yourself. The drawback to this method is you will not get as much exposure to the buyer's market as you would through an agent who would advertise the property on his local multiple listing service(MLS).

If you get an interested party in your property and they qualify to get a home loan to purchase your home, they may be willing to pay enough for the home that you can get some of the equity back in the sale. If they do not offer even the amount that is owed on the home, you can call the lender and see if he will accept the amount they offered as a settlement. If he does, you will have solved your foreclosure problem. If he doesn't you still may be able to negotiate with the lender on a settlement amount somewhere near where the offer was made.

A homeowner must remember that time is a very important factor in the transfer of a property. Once a lender has filed against you, you have only so much time to correct the situation. Even if you have a qualified buyer, or your agent has found one, the transfer of the property and the payment of the debt to the lender has to take place BEFORE the scheduled sheriff's sale date of the property. Most lenders will not delay or call off a sale date posted by the sheriff for your property, because of the expenses, notices and advertising unless there is undeniable proof before him that a transfer is in the process at the time.

An investor, using his or other people's funds can buy a property much faster (but usually for less) whereas a new potential homeowner may have to go through all the procedure at a bank to obtain the loan to purchase.

You have no control over how long that takes and neither does the potential buyer. You can attempt to exert a little better control over this process of him getting a loan by asking your buyer if you can deal directly with his lender regarding the purchase of your home. In this way you may be able to facilitate the flow of documents between the involved parties much easier, set-up and confirm any scheduling needed amongst them, etc.

Deed in Lieu

Another option available to the homeowner facing eminent foreclosure and having tried to sell the property with no success is a deed in lieu of foreclosure. In this particular situation a homeowner voluntarily conveys (gives back) the deed to the lender. This is usually a last attempt by the owner to avoid a foreclosure ending up on his credit record. It will not save the house for the owner, but it does have a slightly less negative impact than actually having the property proceed all the way through the entire foreclosure process.

In return for voluntarily giving the deed to the lender,

the borrower is released of any personal responsibility for the mortgage balance and any future liability or amounts owed including deficiencies resulting from the sale of the home. In fact, this guarantee of release from the debt should be in writing from the lender. If a person cannot secure this promise from the lender, what benefit is there to giving the deed back?

One thing to keep in mind, if considering doing this, is that the property must be free from any other second mortgages or junior liens encumbering it. The lender is not set-up to handle receiving property burdened by other liens, and will refuse the deed if this is the case.

If you are faced with this situation and the property does have another lien on it, it may be a good idea to call the second mortgage or lien holder. Once the foreclosure is filed in the county you live in and the second lien holder can verify this fact, he may be willing to listen to whatever offers you have in mind regarding saving (getting) some/any money for him. This second lien holder knows that if the property does go to sheriff's sale, and if the bid is not high enough, he could lose part or all the money owed to him. That is because debts are paid off in the order they are filed, except for tax debt which has priority over all other debts. When/if the house is actually sold at sheriff's sale all taxes and court fees are paid first, then the remaining amount goes to the first mortgage holder, and if he is paid in full, any additional monies will go to the second mortgage holder, then third, etc. If there is no second mortgage against the property and there was money left over from the sale, this amount would go back to the homeowner.

Assumption

Many times when people get behind on their mortgage they look for a way out of the present situation. One of these ways is to use an assumption.

Basically, you find someone else to assume your loan as it is in place. He brings in the necessary cash to get your loan back on track. You and he can discuss if there is equity in the property, if you should be paid for the equity you have and how. There are many times an assumption can be a good idea, but it can be a double-edged sword.

Beginning the early 1970's most mortgages contain wording in them that state that the loan cannot be assumed by another, or if it can, that the assumption must be approved by the lender.

The lender usually has the new buyer fill out a credit application and reviews him just as if the lender were granting a new loan to him. This process can become complex and time consuming. The lender reserves the right to deny your new buyer the right to assume your loan.

Ideally, the lender will give your new buyer his approval. The lender having gathered all the relevant information necessary, prepares all new documentation that allows the new buyer to come in, catch up the loan, and continue to make the payments as scheduled on the home.

In many situations, the lender will simply qualify the new buyer for a new loan, and give him that new loan for your house. However, if the lender agrees to allow someone else to "assume" the buyer's loan, the homeowner should be sure to get this agreement in writing, and the homeowner should be sure that the lender agrees to release him (the homeowner) from any future liability for the loan.

There are many cases in which the lender will say that he can't release the original borrower on the loan. It is far better to have two parties responsible for the same mortgage than one in the lender's opinion. Don't allow him to keep you tied to the mortgage, especially if he "qualified" the new buyer. There is just no good reason for him to keep you tied to the mortgage. You want to walk away free. If the lender won't allow it, do not proceed with the transaction. It's a call you have to make yourself, but I'd say don't do it. At this point your credit is probably damaged, you've worked with the lender to get a" replacement" and did that. That's leaving the lender in a much better place than most people have.

Outside sources

This is a category to include anything that we have missed or that might occur

Outside sources would include:

Local organizations

Local Churches

Community Organizations

Windfall (lottery) / Gifts

1-888-995-HOPE

Bankruptcy

Bankruptcy is certainly an option to a homeowner in foreclosure. However, it should be a very carefully considered option, and one should not choose bankruptcy just because of an impending foreclosure. Bankruptcy is an all-encompassing solution to tremendous financial burdens throughout your entire financial life including your home.

With a bankruptcy all of your assets, property, shares, anything of real value can be sold to pay your creditors. It also means declaring bankruptcy to deal with non-priority debts puts ALL of the debtor's property at risk. It could put at risk your future assets also. It will definitely have an effect on your future credit, and possibly your employment opportunities, and your housing options. This action should only be taken after serious review and obtaining the advice of a competent bankruptcy attorney.

A bankruptcy candidate would be a person with little or no property, few assets, large consumer debt from national and local creditors, low or no income, large medical bills and perhaps court obligations.

If you decided in chapter 3 that you fit into this category, then by all means get together with a bankruptcy attorney.

Again, the quicker you take action, the better your chances of a favorable outcome being within your control.

To grossly simplify the effect of bankruptcy on a foreclosure is that it temporarily stops the foreclosure. Although it may take away the right of the homeowner being able to sell the property on his decision alone, it certainly affords the opportunity to explore ways to work with the lender, especially in the area of changing the terms of the note and mortgage or "recasting" the loan or in obtaining a reasonable settlement amount if you have procured a buyer. If in the event that all your other obligations was what prevented you from paying on the house, you may to resign (reaffirm) on the existing loan on your home or get another to continue to keep your residence.

Chapter 6
Creative Strategies

Who do I listen to?

We have talked about the standard ideas and practices in regards to foreclosure and what is involved with the procedures in the previous chapters.

Sometimes it seems like no matter who you talk to professionals (agents, investors, or other potential homebuyers), you feel somehow you are not getting the whole story. You are getting their view through their profession and training, which is usually naturally polarized and understandably limited because they are field-oriented and to be good at what they do requires they stay that way.

An attorney is going to give you advice from a legal point of view. I have most often found that attorneys lean toward a very conservative view and almost never entertain telling a client to take a risk in fear that he may fail. It is his job to tell you where and how to avoid risk. But it is your job to decide when you will take the risk. Would you ask your attorney for an appraisal value of your property or a realistic market value based on the current market situations happening in your neighborhood? It's not in his field to provide that. Likewise, a real estate agent is not an attorney, tax accountant or vice versa.

Most real estate agents have their own view. They are convinced if you want to sell it, list it (preferably with them). But when you tell them you are in foreclosure and there is no equity to pay them with, they can't seem to walk away from you fast enough. Many agents will list you with a high asking price and because their commission is based on your selling price, then they will ride on your shoulders into the Sheriff's sale, hoping they can still somehow make money off your misfortune. Shame on their association and their code of ethics for not teaching their agents how to help and work with these foreclosure situations better. I wonder how many homes in foreclosure today were sold by their eager agents pushing to close a deal and get their commission.

I think the more information you have the better decision you can make in any situation. It is only when you get as much information as possible can you clearly see more of the choices and their possible outcomes and try for the best for you and your family. That's why I would say that a good real estate investor has the unique advantage to look at your circumstance from all angles (legal, market, financial) and diagnose it correctly. He has to be aware of all these factors when considering whether to acquire your home or not. His livelihood depends on him being accurate, informed and being able to deal successfully with just the problems you are facing. If you can employ one to act in your behalf during this foreclosure action, you most likely will come out ahead even after you pay the investor a fee to help you make sense of this.

With that in mind, remember this book is being written from the homeowner's point of view, of saving himself from foreclosure and the inevitable credit damage and emotional grief that comes with it. It is the buyer of this book (the homeowner) who's outcome in this foreclosure matter is the most important concern involved here.

If you are living in the property, and you need to stay in it, you will have certain avenues that you must explore to be able to keep your residence, such as renting a part of your home, or renting space (garage). You need to search out the local governmental and non-profit agencies that can help you to negotiate with your lender to allow you to stay in the home. This can be any one of the fixes we discussed earlier in the book, except the liquidation solutions. Utilize whatever inexpensive services that are available before spending money.

If you are being foreclosed on a property that is not your primary residence, or if it is, and you are willing to vacate it to try to save the equity you have in it, you can open many more options for yourself not to lose everything.

I believe there may be many other ways to save yourself. All involve some form of risk just as the standard ideas and practices of foreclosure discussed previously above do. In fact, most things in life involve some type of risk. The idea is to minimize your risk or loss if you can when wrangling out of a possible foreclosure.

Much of your risk will come from those you choose to do business with. Take care when considering bringing in another party to help solve your foreclosure. If you are thinking of leasing out or land contracting your property to someone else or if you are going to allow someone to assume your mortgage, understand that the success or failure of your plan depends on their promise to perform accordingly. In cases like these, choose not from the heart, but with the head, and confirm every fact so you can try to assure yourself of success.

Here are some other facts to examine.

One of these is that you are the owner of that property until the Judge confirms the sale and the new deed is delivered.

When it gets recorded, if you still reside there, the new owner must ask the court to evict you. After this separate procedure which occurs after the deed transfer, then the Sheriff will come to set your stuff on the sidewalk. You being the owner have the authority and control over it till then.

(Technically, you still have some control over it even beyond that point, but that's the attorney's realm to deal with. Ask him about redemption.). You being the property owner have a right to decide if you want to continue owning the property (and continue to derive the benefits thereof) and avoid foreclosure. If so, there are other options. It is your choice. You may choose to make the property pay for itself in some manner. This choice may require someone else to live in the property, but it may allow you continued ownership and save your equity in it.

Realize the problem you are facing with regard to the house is a financial one, not a moral one.

If you can fix the financial aspects, you may be able to get the loan back to a consistently current status (being paid on as agreed) until you can sell the house and pay-off the loan or until all the payments are made, and you or someone else becomes the lien-free, mortgage-free owner.

If you are able to solve the foreclosure and retain ownership of the property, it must be done by either obtaining efficient (new) financing or injecting cash into the current financing. The cash can be provided by you or someone else. The potential to save your equity may also be available to you there depending on your particular situation.

Remember in a foreclosure that time is slipping away. THE FASTER YOU REALIZE YOU HAVE A PROBLEM AND DEAL WITH IT THE BETTTER THE OUTCOME WILL BE. If you are only one or two payments behind, a solution may be far more workable than if you're many more behind. The amount of cash needed to rectify a loan rapidly increases as time goes by (payment, late fee, payment, late fee, etc.).

Find or have in place a good attorney you are comfortable with that will answer your questions from experience. He will also be an excellent choice to negotiate thru to your lender if you need to.

We also mentioned keeping all transactions timed to be finished before a certain date before the Sheriff's sale. Even though a sheriff's sale may be canceled five minutes before it happens, that usually only happens with bankruptcies or in the movies. Don't paint yourself into a corner where you have to play "beat the clock".

One other major factor is the amount of the monthly payment in relation to the property. Can the property earn its own monthly expenses? If so, can I arrange for someone else to pay them for me, at least temporarily, allowing me to retain my equity and credit intact? Can the property generate enough income to pay its own expenses each month and maybe some extra? That "extra" can be your monthly payment for the equity you still have tied-up in the house and couldn't get out until now. What if it doesn't cover it's expenses? Why would I still want it? What if it may even take some of your cash (lump sum or monthly payment), to keep the payments met but in cases where there is rapid appreciation in your market or you have considerable equity in the home that you just don't want to give away, it may be wise to do just that.

If the property has an ever increasing adjustable mortgage payment like so many have today, you will need to refinance into a fixed payment loan, refinance it completely or modify the existing loan terms.

If the payment (principal, interest, taxes and insurance) can be made by the income generated from the property then many avenues for continued ownership can be chosen.

For example, you can move out of the property, and allow someone else to move into and keep the payments current while you still own it by leasing it to them. You can lease it to them for the amount of the payment or more each month depending on the property, and its condition or value. It can be a short-term lease until you are able to again make the payments, or if you are satisfied with the results, you can continue to lease it for a longer term, possibly till the end of the loan if necessary. This allows you to save the equity in the home and maybe after the current phase of mortgage upheaval throughout the industry passes, you may then be able to sell it and recoup the equity left in the house.

You could sell the property in a wrap-around mortgage. This is done when the homeowner (you) creates a new loan, encompassing the existing financing.

For example, the sale of a $100,000 property with a $10,000 cash down payment by the new buyer and a $60,000 first mortgage already in place creates a $30,000 shortage that can be financed by you who would carry back a new wrap around loan for $90,000. This wrap-around would require your new buyer to make the payment on the $90,000 while you would retain the responsibility for making the required payment on the original first mortgage. The difference in the amounts of your incoming payment from your new buyer to you and the outgoing payment on your first mortgage is money for your equity in the property you get to keep. The $10,000 he brought for a down payment can be used to get the first mortgage and/or the second mortgage current again, and if all of it isn't needed to do that, it is your initial installment on your equity in the house. Be wise and keep this extra money in an account in case you need it for the house later.

You could also sell this property to someone on a land contract for a higher amount than what you owe on it, having them make the payments to you, and you sending in the amount owed to the first mortgage holder and keeping the difference each month as your payment for your equity. Again, the new buyer's down payment can get your first mortgage current and back on track. This arrangement can continue until the first is completely paid off and all the payments have been made, then your buyer's payments will be all yours until he pays you for the property in full.

If there is no considerable equity in the property that you are concerned about, you could sell the property "subject to", that is, subject to the existing mortgage that is already in place on the property. You may charge a lump sum fee up front to the new buyer for the right to step-in and take over your loan. Some or all of that lump sum can be used to get the loan current. Remember, it will be your credit that is being risked, because you signed on the loan originally when you bought the house. That aspect will not change until it is paid off or your buyer obtains his own loan. Your buyer will want some guarantee of his eventual ownership of the property once he has made all of the payments. There are many ways to go about securing this for him. One way to do that could be having the deed held in escrow until the final payment is made. This same goal could be accomplished using a land trust. I am sure your attorney knows many more.

Here is another factor to consider when using these actions to prevent your foreclosure. One of these is the due-on-sale clause in your mortgage. It says that if the title to the property is transferred, that the lender can demand that the entire balance can be called due and must be paid in full now. This clause certainly does exist, but let us discuss this for a moment. In today's mortgage atmosphere with foreclosures and defaulted loans at an all-time high, I do not see lender's spending time and money to scrutinize currently good paying accounts looking for possible problems in them. That's not saying that they won't sometime in the future after the housing market stabilizes, but your problem of your foreclosure now may have been long solved by then.

This enables you to get from under the monthly payment quickly and keep control of your equity, or relinquish all of the property to someone else completely if you choose to. You the homeowner can do these things for yourself to a point, and then with the help of an attorney to avoid foreclosure. You can save yourself, your credit, and your family from emotional and financial grief and if managed properly bring about a win-win-win situation for all parties involved.

The benefits of the above described techniques allows you to avoid foreclosure, get some money out of the property that you have put in it and also helps to keep your credit remain in good standing. I think that leaves you far better off than you were when you got your foreclosure notice.

Chapter 7
Life After Foreclosure

You may be able to stay in your home for a long period of time before you must finally have to vacate it. You would have been wise to save those monthly mortgage payments you haven't been making to be used as money to help you find another place to live.

Because you've gotten foreclosed on, you may find that acquiring a new residence to be challenging. Missing mortgage payments can and will affect your credit rating and score in the future if your lender reports this to the credit bureau, and most do. How quickly it is reported and begins to affect your credit depends on several variables, but you will soon notice that you will have a problem obtaining further credit. Lenders will have become hesitant to talk to you about refinancing your current loan on your home or any other loan when they see you have missed some monthly mortgage payments.

You may eventually find yourself looking for another place to live. In any case, if you have some cash saved up for finding a new place to live you will be better off than if you have none. Realizing you cannot go to a bank for another home loan at least for now, you should be aware that there are other ways to secure a place to live depending on your unique and particular situation and lifestyle.

One of those other ways could be to move in with other family members or friends and share the expenses of that household. This idea should not be so quickly overlooked. Depending on your situation this could work out well. A lot is going to depend on your personality and if you can be comfortable sharing your living space. If so, it affords you the chance to save some money, reduce some of the chores such as cooking, cleaning, etc. and also gives you some company when you want it. Granted this arrangement may not be ideal for everyone, but for those who can make the adjustments, it can be a very efficient and inexpensive way to recover from your foreclosure.

You may decide that renting a place is the answer for you. Some landlords are very credit conscious when considering a new rental application and some are not. With so many people facing financial struggles today, landlords who want to fill their vacancies may not fear someone who has been foreclosed on as they once would have. For those landlords who are credit conscious, the best you can do is to be honest with them and explain what happened, and what you are now doing to get beyond that time in your life. Some landlords will accept that we all can fall onto hard times and will allow you to rent from them, some won't.

Your life style may require that you may want to do more than just rent, such as use some of the saved payment money for a down payment on another home via a land contract or a lease option fee on a home. The benefit to this situation is there may or may not be a credit check necessary to participate in a lease-option or land contract situation. If so, then tell them up front before you pay any application fee, that you have a foreclosure on your record and if that is going to be a stumbling block, don't pay the fee to apply. Another way to secure a place to live is thru a lease-option.

A lease-option scenario is where you decide to rent a place for x amount of money per month, and possibly buy the property at a certain time in the future at an already agreed upon price.

In fact, when looking at a potential property to live in, realize that the option fee (the amount used to create the option to buy) and the monthly payment amount are negotiable too. The owner of the property may be asking for terms that you may not be able to meet. Just as in the case of dealing with your previous lender, whatever the two parties agree upon and put into writing will become the new and binding agreement, so use this to your advantage to see if you can tweak your lease-option to make it more appealing and affordable to you.

The same is true for a land contract scenario. The amount of the down payment required to move in and even the monthly payment as well as the sale price, can be adjusted somewhat more enticing from your point of view. A land contract is an agreement to purchase a property for a specific amount. It usually contains a "down payment" which is the initial payment to begin the contract. After the down payment is paid, a buyer (you) continues to make a set monthly payments until the buyer refinances to get a loan to pay off the owner or until all payments are made and the property becomes yours.

The lease-option method of purchasing your next home allows you to "try before you buy", the home and the neighborhood. This method and a land contract purchase enables you to work on part of rebuilding your credit by keeping record of your on-time monthly payments either by saving the cancelled checks or the stubs from the money orders bought to make the monthly payments. This proof of the payments made will become a valuable tool in the future when you attempt to get a home loan again. It will show your ability and reliability after foreclosure to make payments as agreed upon once again.

Whether you are in a lease-option or land contract situation, use the time to improve your credit rating in other ways. It is impossible to start this to soon. Be certain that you make payments to any and all of your existing creditors on time if not earlier. With your credit cards, attempt to pay your balances in full every month. Use them sparingly and wisely so that the result is made to boost your credit score.

After a foreclosure you need to focus on maintaining adequate, steady employment, a satisfactory pattern of paying rent or other (land contract or lease option) payments, and demonstrate good credit responsibility.

These three actions themselves will put you back on the road to revitalize your credit standing although, realize it may take time usually one or two years to get close to where you may have been before the foreclosure.

Chapter 8
Scams

Wherever, whenever there is confusion and money to be made, there are scams (techniques) to make it easier. They were in place when mortgages began, and will be till the end, but you need not to be in one.

This chapter is designed to familiarize you with some of the ways that regular folks are deceived by those who have no ethical standards and are ruthless in their methods. In fact, there are so many different ways to defraud someone that we will list only a few of the most popular techniques.

"I'll buy your house and let you lease from me."

Someone gets the owner to deed (sign over) the house to them usually for nothing or very little money. The new buyer allows the original homeowner to stay in the house and gives him the right to buy back the house within a year or two. The problem is the new payment is the same as or higher than his original payment. If the original homeowner didn't solve or accurately diagnose his own financial problem previously, he is bound to see it occur again. When it does this time, he will find himself being evicted much more quickly as a tenant than when he owned the home as the homeowner.

Dirty lenders

They provide loans to people in financial trouble that "don't fit", that is the loan, the payment plan, or some other aspect of it is certain to bring about its default. Tell tale signs of these kinds of loans are very high loan fees, very high interest rates, and heavy pre-payment penalties.

Always ask what the PITI (principal, interest, property taxes, and homeowner's insurance) payment is, because each month that is what you really have to pay anyway.

"I stop foreclosure"

In this case, companies help you to keep your home for a fee up front.

They call the lenders for you and send in forms you have filled out. In reality all the services they perform you can do for yourself. They may or may not actually talk to the loss mitigation dept., it really depends on how much you stay on top of them to get the job done.

"I'll list and sell" or "I'll buy your house" scam—my personal favorite.

This is usually done by real estate agents and or their brokers. They will list your house for near market value while your sheriff sale date is closing in with the promise to buy it if it does not sell. When it gets apparent that it is not going to sell for the price they suggested you set, and the sale is almost on top of you, they offer to purchase for the balance of whatever is owed to the lender so "you don't have to face foreclosure".

What irks me with this group is they always mention their code of ethics or community service in their advertising, but willingly tie your hands from helping yourself and keep you in the dark as to your other options other than listing. This is the only group "licensed" to kill or screw up with almost no oversight other than a group of their peers.

Equity Skimming

A "buyer" offers to buy your property at just over the mortgage balance, even though there may be considerable equity in the home. You have to move out, sign over the deed to him allow him to deal with your lender. The buyer now rents the property to a third party and starts collecting rental payments.

If he is an ethical individual he will establish and maintain a payment plan with the lender and keep your mortgage current. In fact, he may even get the property sold to the people who move within in a year or two, allowing you to honorably having your loan paid off and still respectably keeping your credit from nose-diving.

If he isn't an ethical individual and doesn't pay your mortgage you continue down into foreclosure, end up with damaged credit and the "buyer" (the guy you signed the house over to) gets to collect a large up-front payment and monthly payments from an unsuspecting tenant at your expense. You can do nothing because you signed your rights away, but you will still be responsible for the mortgage on the home.

I can only say to be aware at all times. Understand what you are doing at each step and know why you need to do each action and where it will leave you. It should leave you in a better situation than you are in now. You may have to give up some things to get you and the family there, but if you weigh each choice at each step, you can navigate your way through it all.

There are ways to avoid each of the scams mentioned above or any variable of it. But you can only defend yourself if you have some knowledge what you are dealing with. Utilize your computer to locate information about these and other scams not mentioned here.

Things to consider

Don't give away the deed to your house without full understanding of why you are doing it. Realize this may or may not relieve you of responsibility of the mortgage if you do.

Review any ideas with an attorney skilled in the area you are asking about (real estate, bankruptcy, foreclosure) that you are comfortable with and with whom you can ask questions and get answers. Ask them what they see to be the pro's and con's of each action you propose to take. However, remember based upon those knowledgeable opinions, you must decide which course of action you will ultimately take.

If you are dealing with anyone calling themselves a buyer, and they want to get you to take action, you have the right to ask them to prove their intentions to purchase by giving you a preapproval letter from their lender or show you proof of the funds that they have in an account to buy your home.

Realize that you will have to be willing to give and take in order to be successful in resolving this problem before foreclosure occurs. Investigate statements that don't ring true. Consider ideas even though they may not be the one you are looking for. Be suspect if it sounds too easy or too good to be true.

Chapter 9
Forms

The next chapter of this book will familiarize you with some of the forms your lender will ask you to complete regardless of which solution you choose. Whether you choose to refinance, modify your loan to lower your payments and/or interest, a forbearance plan, request a short sale, deed in lieu, or any of the other solutions you have learned about in this book, you will be asked to fill out basically the same forms.

You will more than likely be sent a package by fax, email, U.S. mail, or even a courier such as Federal Express or UPS. You will be sked to return the completed forms via the same service as you received them. The following explanations will show you what forms to expect, why each of them is needed and why they are important. Always keep a copy of everything you send for yourself for further reference.

TYPES OF FORMs

LETTER OF HARDSHIP: A hardship letter gives your lender an idea why you have fallen behind on your mortgage. Many times, they are genuine hardships and you have lost your ability to pay. Explaining your hardship allows the person in the loss mitigation department to see you as a person not just a loan number. You may not receive an actual form to fill out, but will be requested to hand write or type an explanation of your particular situation or story. When hand writing a hardship letter, always send supporting documents such as hospital bills, etc. Once again, this allows you to become a person.

FINANCIAL STATEMENT/BORROWER INFORMATION: This information gives the lender an idea of what your assets and liabilities are, what your current income is, and what expenses you have going out each month. This is very important, because it verifies what you are able to do financially to cure your problem. If they can see you are not in the position to cure the problem, or will be financially unable to re-finance or modify your payments, they will be more willing to negotiate a short sale or take the deed in lieu of payment, or one of the other options that don't require you to come up with any money out of pocket to get out of the mortgage.

AUTHORIZATION: An Authorization to release information gives your lender or any of their respective agents the right to gain information regarding credit reports, employment verification, tax information, bank accounts, etc. This information can only be released to them in regards to your specific mortgage with their company. It does not give them rights to your personal information regarding any other matters. It may also give them the right to inspect the property to see what condition it is in.

BORROWER RESPONSE FORM: This response gives the lender, at a glance, an idea of where you stand as far as your current situation with your payments, or what your intentions are to make them or not make them. Your lender is checking for loan viability with this form.

SHORT SALE FORM OR FULL DISCLOSURE AND RELEASE FORM: This form comes into effect if you actually have a person who is willing to buy the property before the foreclosure at a lesser price than the amount due on the mortgage. You and the buyer will sign this to let the loss mitigation department know you actually have a serious buyer with money or financial backing.

LIMITED POWER OF ATTORNEY: This notarized form gives a legal right to a specific person to act as your true and lawful attorney-in-fact for your benefit only regarding the property that is mentioned on the power of attorney. It makes it easier for someone to negotiate with the lender on your behalf without having you present. This is usually not asked for by your lender, but may be asked for if you have another party negotiating with your lender such as a buyer or investor you have found to purchase the property.

SALES CONTRACT: This form can also be called a purchase agreement or sales agreement. It is a legal document signed by you and a buyer stating the terms you are willing to sell this property to a buyer for. These terms will not only include the price, but who is going to pay any escrow fees or closing costs needed to complete the sale of the property and finally transfer the deed from your name to theirs.

REPAIR ESTIMATE: When asking the lender to take a short sale, they will more than likely want to see why they should take less money. Some of the reasons could be because the property has been neglected, damaged, vandalized, or just in poor condition due to age. Regardless of the reason, if you can have a contractor fill out this form, the lender will see all the costs of the repairs needed to bring this property back to an appraisable value.

COMP FOR THE PROPERTY: "COMPS" is a shorter word for comparison. When your lender is trying to make a decision to accept your buyer's offer of a lower purchase price, they want to know what kind of comparison this property has is value to others in the area. In order to appraise a property, certified appraisers have to find houses that have sold in the last year within one mile of that property. They usually have to find three or more properties that are alike, with the same amount of bedrooms, baths and square footage. Then they use those sales prices to estimate the value of your property in comparison. This does not mean you have to pay for an appraisal. You just have to come up with comps for the area.

PROOF OF FUNDS LETTER: When you have a buyer who is offering full price or short sale price, the lender will often ask that buyer show proof that he has the actual cash in hand to buy the property, or the approval of a lender with a closing date for the buyer before they make their decision to stall the foreclosure process.